BY JAMES LEO HERLIHY

PLAYS
BLUE DENIM (with William Noble)
CRAZY OCTOBER
STOP, YOU'RE KILLING ME

NOVELS
ALL FALL DOWN
MIDNIGHT COWBOY

STORIES
THE SLEEP OF BABY FILBERTSON
    AND OTHER STORIES
A STORY THAT ENDS WITH A SCREAM
    AND EIGHT OTHERS

STOP, YOU'RE KILLING ME

THREE SHORT PLAYS BY

JAMES LEO HERLIHY

SIMON AND SCHUSTER • NEW YORK

Copyright © 1963, 1965, 1967, 1970 by James Leo Herlihy
Published by Simon and Schuster, Rockefeller Center, 630 Fifth Avenue,
New York, New York 10020.

First printing

SBN 671-20538-2
Library of Congress Catalog Card Number: 77-107254
Designed by Eve Metz
Manufactured in the United States of America

Laughs, Etc. was first published in Playboy Magazine; Terrible Jim Fitch was first published in Rogue Magazine.

STOP, YOU'RE KILLING ME, a program of three short plays,
was first presented by Dick Duane with the The-
atre Company of Boston at Stage 73, in New
York City, on March 19, 1969. It was directed
by David Wheeler; the production was designed
by Robert Allen; the music was by Boynton-
Devinney; and the lighting by Ray Long. The
cast, in order of appearance, was as follows:

LAUGHS, ETC.
        GLORIA   Saṣha von Scherler
        An apartment in New York's East Village

TERRIBLE JIM FITCH
        LONESOME SALLY WILKINS   Rochelle Oliver
        TERRIBLE JIM FITCH   Larry Bryggman
        A motel room on Route 66, near Albuquerque,
        New Mexico

BAD BAD JO-JO
        KAYO HATHAWAY   William Young
        FRANK   Matthew Cowles
        DENNIS   Phillip Piro
        Kayo's Manhattan penthouse

CONTENTS

LAUGHS, ETC.

For Darwin Porter

Character
GLORIA

Setting: GLORIA's *apartment in New York's East Village. A spotlight illuminates just one small area, which contains an easy chair and a side table.*
Action: GLORIA, *a woman in her middle years, is seated in the chair, speaking to her unseen friends and, at intervals, to her unseen husband.*

GLORIA: Tom, don't you think I should tell Ceil and Harry about Friday night? Well, *I* do.

It was truly one of those I mean like (quote) great nights (underscore). And it came about with no help whatever, it just took place. That's East Village, I mean it's not the East Seventies. Things can still happen here, thank God we moved.

To wit: We have these really darling kids upstairs—three Boys. (Don't ask me what the "arrangements" are!) One of them, the blond, with hair down to here and eyes that see other worlds, is sweet on me. Strictly Oedipus-type thing, I mean it's not *voulez-vous coucher,* he wants to be in my *lap!*

Which I, Gloria of the barren marriage, see no harm in.

Tom, Tom, Tom, I'm not blaming *anybody* for the barren marriage, Ceil and Harry know we've chosen it thus, they know you're just bursting with seed. Pretty please, I'm trying to tell something, Tom, is nothing sacred?

Anyway!

I'm sitting here, gagging with boredom, at ten-thirty Friday night: Tom asleep in that chair, much as you see him now, mouth slightly open. *Very* attractive. Oh, Gloria wasn't bored. She was embalmed!

When *rap-rap-rap* on her chamber door, it's the blond one, Could he have some ice cubes, please. Looking like an archangel and his name is Michael! Can you bear it?

Nor can I.

So, just on an impulse, No, I said, I won't let you have a single cube, but you may have a drink.

Oh but, said he, finger pointing toward Heaven, I have these friends up there.

Ah well, the more angels the better, Go fetch them, I said. And while he was upstairs fetching I telephoned the liquor store.

Oh. Oh thank you, Tom, for that wonderfully salty contribution to my tale. Ceil and Harry are so grateful to hear all about the liquor bill. Now back to sleep, don't exhaust yourself, and we'll just see if I can't somehow manage to limp through without all this detailed assistance.

So.

I no more than hang up the phone when the parade begins. This lovely airborne parade. Angels and archangels. Cherubim and seraphim. All manner of winged creature, lighting gracefully on the furniture.

Slight hyperbole here: there were only three actually. Three Boys.

And this curious girl.

A dreadful little stump of a thing named Jo-Anne. All hair and horn rims. Truly. All you could see was its smock, its little fists, with ud-cray galore under its fingernails, *ça va sans dire*, and the most formidable hair. Virtually you could not see its face without trespassing. I haven't to this day the faintest notion of what the child looked like.

And yet, in retrospect, she managed, without speaking so much as a word that anyone heard, mind you, she saw to it that she became the star of the evening. Truly! This unappetizing little bitch!

Wait! Wait! I have to tell things in my own way.

All right: I know she'd been living up there with The Three, because I'd been seeing her for a couple of weeks, darting about the halls with pathetic little grocery bags. Making Herself Useful, I suppose. It seems Michael the Archangel had found her in the street in front of the Electric Circus one morning at dawn, just sitting there inside of all this hair, and brought her home to make a little sister of her. Apparently they adore having little sisters.

(And mothers, a-ha-ha.)

So at one point, on ze glorious Friday night, Michael follows me to what we laughingly call the bar, that sad little tea wagon there, and wants to know what I think of his Jo-Anne. And I said, Michael, I haven't even seen her yet, what is all that hair about?

He looked at me with these ghost-blue eyes (Ceil, you'd faint!), and he said, perfectly serious, Jo-Anne's in hiding. From herself.

Oh, you idiot, Harry, of course I didn't laugh. What *am* I? Granted, inside, in here where it counts, I was splitting. But not a flicker did I show.

Then Michael said, Gloria, I hope you'll try to bring her out, will ya? Try to get to know her a little? She's very worthwhile, she has all kinds of original thoughts, insights, ideas, she has her own little window on the world.

(Window! I thought; what the poor thing needs is a periscope!)

In any case, I was distinctly uneager, shall we say, to enter that red, unwashed wigwam. Treasure trove or no.

But anyway there we all were, having our otherwise memorable and splendid Friday night: one of the Boys was doing perfectly thrilling things with his hands, an entire puppet show without puppets, *unbelievably* touching. And it was all wonderfully fey.

But a little too much so for Tom. Fey he doesn't mind if it's mixed, *un peu*. So I get on the blower once more and call Tom *deuxième*, who stage-manages at this coffeehouse over here, you know the one, Café Something, off-off-off-*off*-Broadway?

Seconds later in traipses he with the entire cast of this terribly integrated revue. And then Tom, my Tom, Tom *première*, really perks up. Tom likes Africans. Oh, he does he does he does! When I'm suntanned he can't keep his hands to himself. The dark shadow of Mama or something!

Oh look! Look! That brought him to life again! The sound of his own libido always does it. I have the most self-referencing husband in the world, I wish there were a contest I could enter him in.

Back to sleep, tiger.

Well now, with all this utter variety going on all over the place, I think—selfless being that I am—of all my dear square friends uptown. And I want them with me. I want them to see that Life Can Be Beautiful. So, on the blower again, dialing my fingies right down to the knuckles. *Come at once!* I shout to all and sundry; laughs, etc., at Gloria's. And Tom's.

I did call you!

Tom, how many times in all did I call Ceil and Harry? Eight, or was it only twenty?

Well, if people are mad enough to entomb themselves at the cinema on the first really brilliant night of the summer . . .

It was glorious. It was balmy. It was Heaven replete with angels. All you could smell was life—and perhaps a little pot, ha-ha. We threw open that door to the fire escape, every window in the place, even the skylight, and let everyone flow at will.

Talk about heterogeneous! We had everything. Plus

these performers. The talent could kill you! I won't tell you about this one singer, not yet, I'm *saving* that! You'll die.

Where am I, for godsake?

Oh yes, the gnome. Jo-Anne.

At odd intervals throughout the evening or shall I say night, out of the corner of my eye, I catch its little act.

Nothing.

In short, it sits. A perfect lump. Inside of itself. Occasionally Michael goes over to it, puts his angel nose inside this disastrous hair and whispers to it. It whispers back. He puts his arm around it. He takes it to the roof for a breath of air. He guides it across the room to meet someone. He gives it a Coca-Cola.

(*Nota bene*: It doesn't drink hard liquor. Oh, no, not at all, my dears! Nothing so simple! *Wait* till you hear what's coming up!)

Now let's do a little montage of time pressing on: Me, this very matron you see before you, doing a watusi with the puppeteer (and quite good actually); Michael, trying to get his little catatonic to dance; Tom here, trying to get a little something *else* going on the roof.

He didn't hear that, just as well, I'd better whisper: Yes, my Tom, Tom *première, not* cohabiting with Africans on the fire escape, and *not* very pleased about it. No thank you, said Miss Ghana. A stunning thing she was, too, *imperial*, and quite an artist of the put-down apparently. Tom doesn't know I had a full report.

What, Tom? Nothing, baby, you're just sensitive. Now nod off for Mama; that's it.

Isn't he heaven?

So! Emergency time! Michael, the guardian angel of the gnome, backs Mama into the bedroom! Yes, *me!* Too good to be true, surely!

Alas, it *was* too good to be true: he didn't want Gloria, he wanted money.

19

Thirty-five smackeroos. Which is not thirty-five cents, need I add.

Good heavens, Michael, replied I, that's a great deal of money.

Oh, but he simply *had* to have it!

Frankly, he didn't look like he was kidding either, he was white as a sheet.

I said, Michael, are you in some kind of trouble?

No, but a friend of mine is, he said.

(Big light flashes on.)

Jo-Anne? I said.

Yes, she's sick, she's very sick. She's got to have some (and there was ever-so-tiny a pause) some attention! he said. She's got to have some *attention!*

(*Klieg* lights flash on.)

Drugs? I said.

Michael nodded.

H? I said.

H, he said.

And you want *me* to put up the thirty-five dollars to get her through this one?

You've got to, he said.

I've got to? I thought. My back went up. I adore this boy, but I don't *got to* anything of the kind. My poor Tom here works like a Trojan for thirty-five dollars, I felt guilty enough pouring out his good liquor for these greedy young cannibals. Which they swill happily, all the while I'm sure silently putting down Tom for being such a square as to actually practice anything so dreary as the law so he can come *up* with the money to finance a party. For them.

Frankly, it made me cross.

But Gloria did not blow her cool. All she said was, Michael darling, why have I got to? *I* can't afford such expensive vices myself, why must I support Jo-Anne's?

Because she's beautiful, he said. Because she's a human being. Because she's dying.

Dear Michael, I said, get her to a doctor at once if she's dying, don't come to me!

He said, Doctors file reports and Jo-Anne's too young to have her life ruined.

Well, yes, I said, there is a question of legality, isn't there. And you're asking me to involve myself? Please, I urged him, get the girl to a doctor!

(To be perfectly honest, I wanted her out of my house.)

He said he bet I wasn't so worried about legality at income tax time, or when I wanted an abortion. (He had me there! But of course the two things are not comparable!)

In any case he was furious, he absolutely *turned* on me!

Screw doctors, he said, screw cops, screw legislators, screw society! All she needs right now is one human being.

With which he turned on his heel and left the room.

I, of course, was the enemy.

Well, I went into ze dainty powder room and did what I could with a little cold water applied to the face. I'm damned, I said, if my night's going to be wrecked by that hirsute little junkie! Oh, I felt sorry for her, God knows, but there was just one teensy little question: **Whose** problem was it? Mine?

The answer to that didn't seem *too* tricky to me, so I went in and poured myself a good stiff one.

As a matter of fact, I think I'll fill this thing up right now.

Oh, would you, Harry? Thank you. Right to the top, and not too much ice.

No no no, the Scotch, damn it!

I did not shout.

So! Another montage. *Le temps marche,* it's now Saturday A.M., party still in progress.

I only remember seeing Michael once more, he was passing through the dining room saying, Is there a human being in the house, is there a human being in the house—

looking bitter and grave and fugitive from Heaven; and that's the last I saw of him. Until . . .

Oh, but I know what's next: this song thing!

I won't be able to do justice to it, it's one of those things where you have to be there.

But I'll try:

At some juncture or other—I'm none too clear about time sequences—I came out of the bathroom and heard this fabulous silence. Everybody, all these young, wild things, standing stock-still, not uttering a sound. Well, well, wonders me, what's going on here?

Then I heard!

This singer was out on the fire escape. Singing to the rooftops.

You know that song from *Fantasticks*: try to remember a something September when nights are something and something is something else?

Well, this boy, an Italian, one of those three angels from above, with the most glorious tenor voice!

No! No, I'm wrong! *Not* really glorious! *Not* a great voice!

Merely perfect! Perfect for *that* song at *that* moment on *that* fire escape on *that* Friday night.

And everybody knew it. There was this enormous, collective sharing of something truly magical, and not a soul was excluded.

But that's not all. Something happened to top it.

You know where the end of the song goes: *Follow follow follow?*

Well! Just as he got to that part, there was a new voice! A woman's. We don't know where she was. We don't know who she was. We couldn't even see her. She was in some other building, way-way-way across the courtyards, leaning out of some dirty little window I suppose. And when our tenor was through, she picked it up in her sad little penny whistle of a voice; she sang: *Follow follow follow.*

I cried. Me, who doesn't cry any more. I cried. I'm crying now!

Everybody did. It was as if we were all seven again, and pure, and taking our first Holy Communion. Together. There was this feeling of the Oneness of humanity, the sort of thing Dostoevski raved about.

Excuse me, let me blow this nose.

Honestly, Ceil and Harry, I just adore this neighborhood. *So* it's noisy, *so* it's bearded and unwashed, *so* there are no taxis. You *take* all that, because it's alive!

Even if you are held responsible for murdering all the junkies. Don't you love that kind of thinking? It's terribly popular now. Some Negro playwright started it: the claim is that I, Gloria, personally adjusted the rope around every black neck that's been strung up in the U.S.A. for the last four hundred years. And of course it follows that this same dreadful Gloria is responsible for shelling out thirty-five smackeroos to save the life of every drug fiend in Manhattan!

Madly logical, don't you think?

Tom and I are strictly from Squaresville, we happen to think charity starts right here, we sort of look after each other first and foremost, don't we, sleeping beauty?

Never mind, dear, not important.

What?

The girl? Jo-Anne?

Well, I *said!*

Harry, I did!

Didn't I? Well, I know I did, I must have, that's what I've been going on and on about.

Forgive me, then, I *thought* I *said:* the poor little thing did indeed die.

Tom and I felt wretched, as you can imagine.

She died the next afternoon. I guess they were trying to do the withdrawal bit upstairs, you know, home style? And it just plain did not work.

I saw Michael in the hall that evening and he delivered the bare facts, looking—you guessed it, homesick for Paradise—and *so* tragic. And pointedly *not* saying I told you so.

I still adore him. It's just that once in a while he makes me a teensy bit cross.

TERRIBLE
JIM FITCH

For Josemario G. Zayas

Rochelle Oliver as LONESOME SALLY WILKINS *and Larry Bryggman as* TERRIBLE JIM FITCH *in* Terrible Jim Fitch

Characters
TERRIBLE JIM FITCH
LONESOME SALLY WILKINS

Setting: An inexpensive motel room located on Route 66, near Albuquerque, New Mexico. It is daytime, but the window shades are drawn so that it appears to be night. The most prominent piece of furniture in the room is an iron bedstead, but there are also a vanity table and bench, a chest of drawers and a chair. The arrangement of personal belongings might indicate that the inhabitants are used to making themselves at home in temporary places. On the floor near the bed is a small wooden ukulele painted blue.

Action: SALLY WILKINS *comes in, leaving the door wide open. She wears a slouch hat, a trench coat and high-heeled shoes. Her face is partly hidden by the brim of her hat and by the turned-up collar of her coat. It is clear from her general attitude that she is in a depressed state. She goes to the vanity table and sit motionless in front of the mirror. After a moment she reaches into a drawer and withdraws a jar of cold cream, removes the lid and begins to smear the mirror with white. But this project cannot hold her interest for long. She leaves it undone, slowly wiping her fingers with tissues. After another motionless moment, the bed begins to claim her attention. She seems to lean toward it, drawn by it.*

A man appears in the open doorway, carrying a six-pack of beer. Unnoticed by the woman, he watches her movements. This man is JIM FITCH. *He wears vaguely Western clothing, appears to be a kind of cowboy—but as the play unfolds there arises some question as to where he would be most at home, in the saddle or on Times Square. He has a wild aspect, this* JIM FITCH, *like a creature someone tried to tame by cruel methods that failed. He is sometimes a little punchy, but always on the alert for treachery from others; at moments he is extravagantly joyful, as if dazzled by the miracle of his own survival. His own habitual attitudes are at the moment suspended as he watches the woman. Slowly she rises, and like one surrendering to a power more considerable than her own will, she goes to the bed and lies on it. Now* JIM FITCH *carries the unopened beers to the dressing table. When he has looked for a moment at the mess of cold cream on the mirror, he take a drink from the can in his hand, and speaks.*

JIM FITCH: The manager of this motel just asked me if something was wrong with my woman. I told him to shut his goddam mouth. Then I figured what the hell, so I grinned at him—you know how I do, tee-hee?—and made out like I was joking. And I said no, everything's fine, thank you, my woman is a little down in the dumps here of late, but it'll pass. Then he started in talking about a slew of women he knew of. And they was all down in the dumps, all forty-four hundred of 'em.

I wanted to tell him to shut his goddam mouth all over again. But I just walked away.

Anybody want me to open 'em a can of beer?

Why, there's Lonesome Sally Wilkins, over on the bed!
And what's this?

>(*He picks up the ukulele.*)

Why, I believe it's—yes it is—it's her blue ukulele!
I wonder if she'll talk to me.

>(*He goes to the bed, leaning on the iron bed-
stead, and looks down at her, speaking with great
and real tenderness.*)

Lonesome Sally. I am returning to you your blue ukulele.
I love you, Lonesome Sally. Terrible Jim loves you to
death. Yes he does. You want me open you a can of beer?

>(*No answer from* SALLY. JIM *walks back to the
dressing table.*)

I'm gonna open Sally a can of beer.

There! I have opened her a can of beer.

Hey, pretty thing. I'm holding a can of beer out to you
here.

Well, I'll just set it here for you on the floor, for when
you want it.

>(*He places the beer on the floor next to the bed.*)

He asked me, the manager of this place, he asked me if
you was some famous person. I suppose 'cause you're so
pretty and your heels are so high and your hair's so lovely,
you must've put him in mind of some famous person. I
can't blame him thinking that. Shoot.

I said, well, technically no, my woman is not world-
famous, but she knows how to walk into a saloon and put
the jukebox out of business. And she was on the radio once
in Brownsville, Texas. Sang one little song on her ukulele,
and five minutes later the switchboard was jammed with
people calling up, inquiring. And for years after, the post-
cards was still rolling in, all of 'em wanting to know who
was the owner of that lonesome, beautiful voice that sang
"When My Blue Moon Turns to Gold Again." Well, I
told him how I give that Brownsville radio station permis-
sion to announce that the singer in question was a lovely

33

lady name of Lonesome Sally Wilkins. *But!* Sad as it may be for the public at large, Lonesome Sally was now the personal and private property of one Jimmy K. Fitch of Decatur. I—uh—went on to admit that this Jimmy K. Fitch was pretty much of a no-account, with a criminal mentality to boot, and clearly, he don't deserve to be the only person in the whole wide world nowadays that gets to listen to the voice of Lonesome Sally Wilkins singing songs on her blue ukulele.

But he is.

Yes, I told the manager of this motel—this person, this Terrible Jim, gets any song he wants any time he wants it: "Oh Careless Love," "Too Late to Worry, Too Blue to Cry," "I Can't Stop Loving You," "When My Blue Moon . . ."

(*The woman turns over.*)

Did you think I was asking you to sing me a song now? I am merely repeating to you a conversation I had with the manager of this motel. And you, you thought I was asking you to, ha, to sing me a song?

Well, you're wrong. You just don't listen to a person. You sure don't. If I was in the mood to hear a song, you would know it, they wouldn't be any guesswork about the thing. I'd say, All right, Sally, I want "The Streets of Laredo," and you'd take up that mother- . . . (*indicating the ukulele*) . . . and you would goddam well pick out "The Streets of Laredo" on it. And you would sing, lady, yes you would, no matter what mood you was in, hear me? You understand? Yeah, I think you do.

What I'd like to hear now, I'd like to hear the sound of that ukulele cracking over . . .

Agh, to hell with it.

(*At the window*) In case anybody thinks I am crazy about this weather—well, I'm not! I don't like it any better out there than I do in here. So what chance have I got?

(JIM *takes a swallow of beer, looks at the can with disgust.*)

Aaagh, I hate this stuff. I've lost m'taste for beer altogether. Drink it more to keep m'throat wet than anything else, purely a matter of maintaining some level of bodily humidity, but they's no pleasure in it.

(*He lights a cigarette.*)

Same with these damn things. I hate 'em with all my heart. Love lighting 'em up, striking the match, blowing out the flame, up to there I'm fine. But after one puff, the whole thing goes kerflooie on me.

That takes care of beer, cigarettes. What else is there, food? I am fed up with food, too. I am fed up with practically anything you can name. Fed up with the weather, fed up with this room, fed up with you, fed up with New Mexico and new this and new that—'cause it's all *old*.

I am fed up with breathing. Look at this! Take it in, let it out, take it in, let it out; Christ, I wish I could think up a substitute for breathing; I'd make a million dollars.

(JIM FITCH *settles into a chair.*)

Sally. I opened a can of beer for you. I set it there for you, on the floor.

Now, um, if you was to reach out with your, uh, left arm, keeping it horizontal and parallel to the bedstead, that is at a ninety-degree angle to your own body, then lower it, I'd say eleven inches, eleven and a half, and wiggle your middle pinky—well, I believe you'd get it wet. Go ahead. Then lick it off and see if that don't give you the taste.

Trying to make things easy for you today, little lady. Hence, the highly detailed, precision instructions on how to get at that beer with a minimum of effort.

Don't care for that plan? Well, now, let's give it some more thought then. Seems to me with my *criminal mentality* I ought to be able to come up with something here. How would it be if I was to come over and hand it to you? Or pour it down your gullet for you?

Don't care for that either, do you? You don't seem to have a whole lot to say here lately, do you, little Sal, my pretty gal? Is that some kind of a new wrinkle? I guess you're fed up, too, is that it? Fed up with conversation, fed up to the point where you don't even grunt any more?

That kind of worries me.

And tell the truth, I'm a little worried about that hat staying on, too, and that hair pulled over y'face like that. Now, when we come in the door here, I fully expected to see that hat come off, and the coat, too. I didn't even give the matter much thought. I just fully expected them garments'd be removed as a matter of course! But that is not what took place here; no, not atoll. What took place was you just kept yourself covered up. That surprised me. I'm gonna be honest about this thing; it hurt me. It hurt me! I suppose I have somehow always pictured myself as the kind of a simple-ass son-of-a-bitch a person could show his face to, isn't that a laugh?

You going to keep your collar up forever? And your hat pulled down forever? I am opposed on principle to anybody going around hiding his face, especially forever.

Sal, the thing you don't realize is, it just calls attention, more attention. Person'll think, what's the matter with that fine-looking woman, collar pulled up and hat yanked down that way? They don't know you're merely hiding a couple weensy little scars. No, Christ no, they put their minds to work on it, and they figure you must be hiding about four hundred big purple sores with green pus coming out of 'em. A person's mind has got this tendency to make things worse than what they are. You follow my point or not?

Take that waitress. Back at the drive-in? Her mind was on fire, couldn't you tell? She was itching to get a good squint at that face of yours. What you think she was hanging around for, making all that jackass conversation?

Now you might think she was on the make for me. Well, she was, that's only natural. But that was just the half of it. The other nine-tenths of her was praying to Jesus she'd catch you off guard and get one good healthy eyeful.

(*He walks over to the bed.*)

I'm going to set down here and I'm gonna tell you the truth: I believe you look better with them scars. Fellow look at you now, he'll think, Hey, that beautiful lady is nobody to fool with! Whereas, before, frankly, you could've been mistaken for some kind of a pushover. Pretty as hell, but possibly a pushover. Hear me? Sal?

Sally! Did you shiver? You shivered. Oh. Oh. Oh my God. That's the first time my Sally ever shivered from me just saying her name. And I said it nice. I know how I said it; I know all about saying a person's name, they's a thousand ways to do it. You can make it like "*Sally!*" Like a knife you're trying to cut 'em up with. But that's not how I just done it. I went at it easy. Should've made you feel like I was rubbing your back: "Sally darling," I said.

Didn't I?

Hey, are you listening to me?

I said, are you hearing me?

Uh, listen here, Miss Lonesome, I am sorry you got your face messed up. I am damn sorry you got your face messed up. It's an awful goddam pity it had to happen. But mark you, baby, I am Jimmy K. Fitch and I am the same Jimmy K. Fitch I was last week; and Jimmy K. Fitch rhymes with son-of-a-bitch, and that means when I talk I like to see ears quiver.

(JIM *goes to the dressing table for a fresh beer.*)

Maybe you'd rather have a Coca-Cola, you want a Coca-Cola? There's a machine in the office.

Oh, I guess you think I'm a pretty terrible person. Terrible Jim, is that it? Mm-hmm, yeah, uh-huh, I know, all my life I been terrible. That's what they all called me in Decatur. Hit that town from Arkansas when I was thirteen; and right from the start, every mama in town would say to her kid each morning, "Don't let me catch you playing with that Terrible Jim Fitch." They all said that.

Every mama but my own. My own mama never called me nothing worse than darling. "Good morning, darlin' Jim, come here to me."

Hug.

"Hey, darlin' Jim, I brought you a present from Cincinnati; close your eyes." You see, my mama was a hooker just like you, but she knew how to say darlin' to a man and make it stick. Last time I heard that voice I was thirteen and it was on the telephone from St. Louie. She said, "I am coming' to fetch you in the morning, darlin' Jim. Bye." So I got into my drawers and set up on the front porch all night. But . . .

It's just as well she never come for me, never found out what kind of reputation I was beginning to enjoy. Reputation, hell, it wasn't nothing short of fame. I was famous through there, Sal. Southern Illinois, all through there I was famous. I got a kick out of it, too. I enjoyed it.

'Cause, see, I got this *criminal mentality* where I enjoy being called a terrible person. You didn't know that? Oh, yeah, it's a fact. I was told that. By a woman't claimed she was crazy about me, too. A very, uh, religious woman, very intelligent, too, knows all about Jesus and psychology and Heaven.

(*He is referring to* SALLY.)

Well, it was her said I had this thing, *this criminal mentality*. Said my case was extremely extreme, which accounts for why I like to rob churches. Can you fancy that, Sally? Here I always thought I liked robbing churches 'cause they was easy. But it turns out that's got nothing to do with it. *Why?* she says, *why* is it robbing churches is so easy for you? Well, I said, because they's nobody tending 'em! No no on, she says, the *real* reason!

I wanted to puke.

Wonder how it is that somebody's supposed to be so

crazy about you can just set around thinking up dirty words for you. Makes you feel lonesome.

But I got no cause to be lonesome, not any more. 'Cause nowadays and henceforward, they's two terrible people around here, one with this terrible mean streak in him, me, and one with the terrible fa- . . .

(*The withheld word is face.*)

I didn't mean that the way it sounded, kid, not by a long shot.

Sal, listen to me, you are one good-looking gal, always was, always will be. I am proud to be traveling around with such a good-looking gal. All I meant when I said terrible was . . .

Sal, I'm going to have to be truthful about this thing: you was getting *too* perfect there for a while, you was getting too pure. That's all right for a little virgin to go around looking like a bunch of buttercups, but when that little virgin gets to be a woman—and a hooker to boot; yeah, hooker—then something's got to take hold of that face and give it a little—a little something to show she knows how to take her lumps.

Ex-hooker?

Oh. No kind of hooker atoll any more, is that it? Not even ex?

Well! That's a crying shame, 'cause the lady I took a tumble for was a hooker lady. And a damn fine one. Are you not that lady? Did I not meet you in the passion pit at the Lavender Fawn in Key West, Florida? Or are you some other lady altogether? Let me see your face.

Oh, Lord, 'scuse me, I said "face" again, didn't I!

Shoot! This won't do atoll. We got to get you straightened out, Sal. We got to get you pulled together. We got to initiate some kind of rehabilitation program. We got to assist little Sal in getting accustomed to showing her face.

What we'll do, we'll go out and find us a crowd of people. Maybe drive in to Albuquerque. To the bus depot.

They's always a crowd of people in the bus depot in Albuquerque. You ought to know, you used to work it.

(*For a moment, he seems to be overtaken by some vaguely disturbing memory.*)

Now, um, where was I in my thoughts here. I had something I was driving at. The bus depot, the bus depot.

Oh! I know! Program; now listen: we go there. And that hat with the wide brim, you leave that in the damn Ford, *outside*.

(SALLY *instinctively raises her hand to her face.*)

And your hands, you'll put them in your pocket and leave 'em there. Then I'll just march you right into that bus depot, in the heart of downtown Albuquerque, with that fine face poking right out in front of you. And you'll stand there. And you'll let 'em look at you. Just like before.

Know what you'll find? You'll find 'em looking at your pretty eyes, and your pretty hair, and your pretty legs, just like they always did. I swear to it. I swear to you the women'll be wishing they was you; and the men'll be trying to puzzle out how they can get next to you, exactly like before. And I'll bet you my half interest in that Ford out there not one person will pay the least attention to them puny, pathetic, weensy little scars.

And if they do . . .

Listen, Sal, here's what. While you're standing there, in that bus depot, guess where I'll be. I'll be just kind of inconsequentially setting on a bench, not more'n twenty foot away, see? And not paying the slightest attention, hell no, not even looking—'cept out of the corner of my eye. And I don't have to tell you, do I, that I see more out of the corner of my eye than most folks see out of a frigging binocular?

So! I'll be setting on this bench. Waiting. The first mother's son that lowers his big-ass orbs for one split second on them scars of your and wiggles so much as an eyebrow . . .

What can I say, Sal, what can I tell you? That person, that poor unfortunate and extremely unlucky mother is going to run straight into Mr. Ruthless Awful Terrible Old Me. Oh, I could cry, could cry right now, for that poor, poor person, whoever he be, be he white or black or pink, that looks at your scars for one split fraction of an infinitesimal scrap of a goddam unhappy second. Well, I tell you what I probably be forced to do.

I be forced to put him on the floor. Somehow. Neat. And then I'll lift up this big foot, and I'll take that poor mother by the face and . . .

> (*The unspoken words: "and grind it into him!"*)
> (Jim *is stricken with regret for a memory he has evoked. There is a long pause in which the mood changes entirely. He is utterly lost for a moment until he finds himself suddenly in anger.*)

Get up, Sal. I want you up off that bed. Now.

> (*And then compassion.*)

Na, hell, you don't have to get up. Today.

Today I'm gonna let you lie there. Not gonna make you talk either. 'Less you want to of your own accord.

I want to do the right thing by you, Sally. 'Cause you just had one hell of a shock to your system. When a person gets messed up and then he takes the bandages off and gets a good squint at hisself in the mirror, well, it's some shock. To his system. So today, you just do as you please.

Me? Oh, poop, Sal, it don't matter what I do, I'm all right. (*At the window*) The sky has been going all day long from all blue to all black. One minute seems like it might be studying to rain, next minute the sun's up there going tee-hee tee-hee; shee-it. I'm staying put, staying right here with my gal.

I believe I'll play the radio.

No, I'm damned if I will. Twenty-five cents an hour, why that's just thievery. They get you in here on a rainy day, see, and they shove this coin box at you, paint it bright red, look, see that? Bright red. And they figure you'll either jam it full of quarters or go nuts! Well, to hell with them.

(*He kicks it.*)

Sal? Sally. I hope you didn't fall asleep on me.

(*He forces one of her eyes open with his thumb.*)

Hell, I knew you hadn't done that to me. 'Cause you know how I hate that, to talk and not be heard.

Listen, Sal, screw the radio. Any time I get in a pinch, or trapped somewhere, or waiting on the rain to quit, I make use of my time; I am a man with inner re-sources; I got m'philosophy to work on. Believe it be a good day for it, rainy.

All great men do that, you know: Beethoven, Einstein, what they do, they figure out a system. Now the general run of people think philosophy is something complicated, and deep. Nah, not atoll. Philosophy is nothing but a system of angles you figure out to keep from going nuts in some motel room. It's all in the world it is.

I ever tell you about my friend Silas in San Pedro? Silas was not a composer. Actually he was a pimp. And a fine man, never nervous about anything. Now Silas was a man with a system. Trouble was he was part Indian, and Indians don't talk much so I never did learn what his system was. I believe it had something to do with smoking marijuana.

That don't work for us though, does it, Sal? We just get hungry. Every time you and me light up, we start in eating like a couple horses and acting a fool.

(*He laughs, stopping abruptly.*)

Person's got to have some system. There was a while I thought I had me one. Come to me in a dream.

How it happened was, I got in a fistfight one night in Key West. Got *my* face all mashed up that night. And when I went to sleep . . . no, it wasn't night, it was daylight; and I was sleeping in the back seat of a car. I don't know whose car it was. Some stranger owned that car.

Now, um. Now, goddammit, I'm losing my point.

What am I talking about, Sal, something about sleeping in cars? Help me!

Answer me, goddam you. . . . Some day, some day, lady, you are not gonna answer me, and God help—

I got it! Sleeping in cars! One night in a saloon in Key West, I got in a fistfight and when it was daylight I went to sleep in a car and had this dream about philosophy. There! I remembered—without anybody helping me.

Now, the dream: I dreamt I was sleeping not in any back seat, but in a great big mother-grabbing room, and in this room was every son-of-a-bitch in the world. I mean every man woman and child, black white and yellow, and every wild tiger and every little puppy dog and every god-dam grasshopper. That room had everything that's alive in it.

And you know what we was doing? Me and all them Chinamen and old ladies and all them animals and kids and insecks, et cetera? We was in there praying together; eyes closed, setting still, and praying. Can you imagine that, Sal, me with my criminal mentality, having a dream about praying?

Well, here's the twist; we wasn't praying to God, no, not by a damn sight! We was praying *about* Him. We was praying He wouldn't get us. Yeah, you heard me. We was all in there, in this big room, and He was outside coming at us, God; and the way it was: one at a time, He could take us—but if we stuck together, He couldn't. See? So all us live creatures was banded together in that room, safe. It was the sweetest damn dream, Sally. It was like—uh, Sal, do you remember sucking on your mama's titty? I do. I remember drinking my mama's milk; and that's how the dream was. Safe and sweet. They wasn't anybody gonna grab your ass. Not even God. 'Cause like I said, if we stayed together, God was gonna quit bugging us. He was gonna cool it. He was gonna turn the misery valve down for a change; flip the lonesomeness switch off. No more bad news; no more bad dreams; no more sleeping alone; or with a cold woman. All that crap was gonna cease!

I woke up thinking I had me a system. And I was tickled pink, too. Face bleeding, nose busted, one eye swollen shut; but I had the world by the short hairs! 'Cause I knew this secret: get everybody to stick together and God will let up on you.

Well, let me tell you, that little notion about cost me my butt; they wasn't a one soul I told it to but thought I was trying to put something over on him; or else I was some kind of mental defective.

You see, if you got a system depends on everybody in the world agreeing with you—forget it. That system is no good, it is worth exactly zero. What you got to have is a kind of system that works when you're all alone.

And they's only one little bitty hitch; they's no such animal.

Listen to me, Sal. I'm experienced. I been on the road all my life, and I state flatly—when you're all alone, they isn't nothing works.

Oh, you poor thing, you think you got it so bad, don't you, traveling around with terrible me, just 'cause I'm a little mean once in a while; just 'cause I messed up your face a tiny bit.

Well, there's one thing even worse can happen to you: you just go on out on that road—alone. Go. Go ahead. I'll let you take the Ford, it's yours.

Here, I'll even pack your damn suitcase. Here's your panties, here's your brazeers, here's your cashmere sweaters. Your war paint, your cold cream, your eyelash curler. Here's your *eyelashes!*

And half the money. I'm putting it in your pocketbook. I believe you'll find a good hundred and fifty in this wad; that ought to be enough, Sister Sal, to get you to the nearest, uh, convent.

And here is one blue ukulele.

And the car keys. Yeah. I give you the Ford. And I give you the open road, and I say go. *Vaya con Dios* all by yourself alone and see how you like that awhile.

Well. Why don't you move? You got my word of honor I will not move a finger to stop you. I know you don't take much stock in the word of honor of a person with a criminal mentality, but here's a good time to try me.

> (SALLY WILKINS *sits up and looks at the suitcase with her pocketbook, the ukulele, and the car keys on top of it. After a moment, she allows herself to fall back on the pillow.* JIM FITCH *is clearly relieved. When he speaks, it is with complete sincerity.*)

I'm glad you decided to stay. 'Cause I'd miss you something awful.

But they isn't nothing going to change much, you know that, don't you? As long as you're with me, you'll be living on the net proceeds of my church work. I'm too old now to change my style, Sally. Some people part they hair on the right, some on the left. Well, I don't part my hair atoll. I rob churches. Oh, when I was younger I used to think about it plenty, other ways of making a living. And I've tried 'em. I've hustled, I've pimped, I've pushed, I've conned, I've done stores and private residences, all them things. But I am a church man. Hardest thing in the world for me is pass up a church. I just got to try the door, and if it's unlocked—that poor-box is a goner.

Did I ever tell you about the time in San Antone I run into some nuns in my work? Well: one time in San Antone, I was working St. Something-or-other's. St. Cecilia's? I don't know. Anyway I heard this noise. Sound like it was coming from the basement of the church. So I thought I better investigate. And I went in the back and found the stairs and went on down. And there was these two little nuns setting at a big table. Must've been a Monday morning, 'cause they was opening collection envelopes. One of 'em was real pretty and she was busy with the scissors cutting off the ends of the envelopes and dumping the money out on the table. Folding money too, most of it. And the other'n, the ugly one, was counting it up and writing in a book. Well, I couldn't believe my good fortune. I just stood there, astounded. Finally the nuns looked up, and we stared at each other for a while. Then this little cute one said, "What do you want?" And I said, "Well now, sister, since you ask, I believe I'd like to have some of that money." Then the other one spoke up, Sister Mary Ugly, and she said, "This money belongs to God." So I said, "Let me take it to Him, honey; I know a real good shortcut." And I walked over and I gathered up about three hundred dollars, couldn't have been easier, it was like picking dandelions. When I was leaving, the cute one said, "Aren't you ashamed of yourself; you look like such a nice man." "Oh, sister," I said, "I am a nice man. Why, I go to church ever' day of my life." Course, I don't suppose she caught the humor of that.

Neither do you, huh?

That's too bad. Cause what I'm doing, I'm trying to keep this motel room, these walls here, from putting the squeeze on the both of us. Figure as long as I keep talking, we won't neither one of us bust out of our heads. These motel rooms, Sally, they're dangerous you stay in 'em too long.

Hey, let's go find us some space.

I never had a room yet was big enough. Sally, I think I be perfectly to home and cozy in a goddam cathedral! How come is it I always end up in some smelly little closet of a place like this?

I believe this room is gaining on me.

(*He cocks his head, as if listening for a voice in the silence.*)

Yeah. Yeah, it is. Oh Lord. And I think my voice is about give out, too.

Baby, it is time for you to talk. Now I am a rational

animal, and I am talking quiet and simple and logical: we
got an emergency here. You pick some subject fast. Anything under the sun, cabbages and kings, or how it was
when you was a little girl; or eeny-meeny-miney-moe; or
about your daddy dying. Hey, you can tell me all about
your daddy dying if you want to. But talk.

I need the sound of a voice.

Sally! Are your lips moving?

Are you trying to say . . .

No.

No, I don't believe it.

I can't believe it.

The woman is praying. The woman is actually talking—
to God. I think I'll beat her up.

Why, they must be a million people all over the world
yapping at Him right this second, singing at Him, mutter-
ing at Him, ten thousand church organs pumping away,
forty thousand pianos and a million tambourines. Now
you'd think, wouldn't you, that he could leave me alone
with my one little woman and a seven-dollar ukulele
painted blue?

Nope. No, the Good Father wants it all.

Yeah! The Good Father.

Well, you go 'head and pray. While I tell you a few
things about that Big Buddy of yours: I believe His reputation is just ever-so-slightly out of whack with the facts. I'll
go farther. I'll say the only thing halfway to His credit is
Him making the world to be such a pretty place. But not
for you to look at, and not for me to look at. Nah, baby,
we're just people, and people are too scared and ornery to
see straight; it's for Him, for Hisself to look at—way up
there away from the stink and misery: floods, train wrecks,
wars, starvation, diseases, the heat and the cold and the
lonesomeness. Yeah, that's His style: set the place on fire
and scoot off to Heaven to enjoy the flames. You honest
and true think if I pull that kind of crap they going to

come around to me lighting candles and singing songs? Yeah, I bet.

But He don't have to follow His own rules: nope. He give your daddy cancer and what you do? Fell on your knees and got religion, didn't you? And then I come along. And for awhile I believe you like me even better'n you liked Him. Maybe you thought I was meaner. I'm not. Oh, I'm mean; but I can't hold a candle to that One.

Funny: I'll bet you're lying there right now thinking about how sweet it's gonna be in Heaven—away from Terrible Jim. What a laugh; sweet? With Him runnin' it —that ukulele-grabber? Suppose, when you died, Sal, you found out Heaven was just another Albuquerque. What would you do, would you vomit? Know what I'd do? If I died and found out Heaven was just another Albuquerque? I'd go to the bus depot and get me a ticket to Hell, express. Yeah, I think I get along better with the devil running things, thank you. He's probably just some poor old pimp—like my friend Silas in San Pedro. Him and me always got along okay. So I'll get on a bus to Hell. Which will probably be another San Pedro—or Times Square or Tia Juana or Dallas—and I'll make out all right. I can make out in places like Hell: I've had practice.

But not you, you're studying for something sweet and lovely, bands playing, angels on the march. Baby, I hope for your sake they's a real Heaven somewhere, and I hope it's halfway decent. Just look at you, all alone and miserable, praying for help from that deaf old thing up there.

If I was God, I'd hear you.

Know what I'd whisper to you? I'd say, "Hey, you down there, Sally Wilkins, all scrunched up hiding herself on that bed in the Wild West Motel, Route 66, U.S.A. This is God talking. I see you. I hear you praying. You lonesome thing. And I got a answer for you. Just lift up your hand, or one little pinky of it, and beckon to that big snake of a man there, that what's-his-name Jimmy K. Fitch that loves you so. And he'll rush right on over to you, and he'll lie down with you, and you just forget all about that criminal-mentality crap, and you let him give you something good.

"And after, you take up that little uke, pick out some-thing blue on it, and let him listen to it with you. And that'll be what Heaven's like. Almost."

(*In his own voice*) Baby, if you want to, you can tell me how sore you are at me. You may have some grudge. Who knows, you may still blame me for your face; you may not realize I am constitutionally unable to hear bad things about my mentality. Well, you just say so, it's open season, anything at all is hunky-dory—just so it's out loud where I can hear it.

You know, I am none too crazy about certain facets of my own personality. If I could, I'd get rid of 'em. If I could. Take this mean streak of mine. Now, if I knew where that was located in me—say it was a vital organ, a heart or a kidney or a lung, and I knew where it was—I'd take this knife, and I'd cut it right out of me. Yeah, mm-hm, I would. The blood would be squirting and it would hurt like holy hell; but I would keep on cutting till it was all gone, keep cutting it out of me till what was left was a—a nice person. I would do that.

And then you would set up and you would look at me. And you'd say, "Hi, Jim darlin."

And I'd say, "Hey! Sally darlin'."

And you'd say, "Let's get out of this awful little room, let's go to Mexico."

And I'd say, "Wh-wha-what's that, kid? Mexico? You want me to take you to Mexico?"

And you'd say, "Yeah, Jim, I sure would like that, darlin'."

And I'd say, "All right, hell, I can afford it. I got half the building fund for the First Methodist Church in Santa Fe right here in my pocket, I'll take you wherever you want to go. You want Mexico, let's go to Mexico. We'll just wind up the Ford and *phhhhht* right on down and get lost there,

South of the Border. If I got sleepy at the wheel you sing that to me, will you? "Down Mexico Way—that's where I fell in love . . ."

I beg y'pardon? Oh, yes, yes of course.

(*He takes the ukulele and places it in her hand.*)
Mm. That's nice.

(*He hums.*)
Lovely.

Just a tiny bit louder.

Sal.

Sally, honey.

(*Singing*) I wonder what's become of . . .

(*An angry shout*) SALLY!

(*She pushes the ukulele away from her and it falls to the floor.*)
Hey now, that got you, didn't it? Only thing is, it hurts my throat to holler, I'm so hoarse already.

So you talk up now. And you tell me what it is you're holding out for.

Just what is it you want?

Now you're gonna have to give me a clue.

Is it got something to do with this knife?

Lord, I suppose that manager out there was smarter'n he thought he was, asking me if something's wrong in here. I believe he was right. I believe they's gonna be some bad news come out of this room today, here in the Wild West Motel, big bad news.

The lady wants me to kill her.

And I'd do anything for this lady; wouldn't I?

But kill her? Lord, I don't believe I'm in the mood for that.

I wish I had a cat or a dog or something small to warm up with. Here! I believe this ukulele'll do. Let's see here now.

(*He smashes the ukulele against the bedstead.*)
Sal. I killed the ukulele.

Will that do?

Can I stop now?

Please?

Come on, Sally, let me quit now.

I'm beggin you. What's my name? Just say what my name is. You don't have to call me darling with it, but just say that one thing. Say my name.

Once.

BAD BAD JO-JO

For Joe Frazier

Characters

KAYO HATHAWAY

FRANK JONES

DENNIS

Phillip Piro as DENNIS, *Matthew Cowles as* FRANK, *and William Young as* KAYO HATHAWAY *in* Bad Bad Jo-Jo

PHOTO BY EILEEN DARBY

Setting: KAYO HATHAWAY's *penthouse in Sutton Place. There is evidence everywhere of* KAYO's *imminent departure: packing crates, disorder, etc. Prominent on one wall is a large lobby poster for a movie,* Bad Bad Jo-Jo. *Its illustration shows a little old lady with tiny eyeglasses and sensible shoes leading an enormous apelike young man by a chain. The young man wears an Uncle Sam hat that is too small for him.*

Action: KAYO HATHAWAY *is lying on a chaise longue, having a nightmare. We see its effects upon him, slides showing scenes of mayhem and violence, the flashing of a strobe light, and we hear loud, acid-rock music, as he squirms and gasps, reacting to the dream-menace. At length, he recognizes one of the sounds as the telephone bell, and slowly, agonizingly, comes awake. Music ceases as lighting becomes normal, late-afternoon daylight.* KAYO *scrambles toward the telephone like a person accustomed to using it as an instrument of deliverance.*

KAYO: Hello? Hello? Hello? (*He hangs up and looks about him, still frightened, and then dials a number.*) Roberta? Kayo. Was that you? Did you phone me? Just now. Oh. Well then, it was someone else. I was having

the most ghastly nightmare when the phone rang.
Who could it have been? It must have been Seymour.
I thought sure you'd be phoning me to hash over last
night. Oh, I loathed it, Roberta. And when I think
it was my own farewell party! I'm so depressed. Do
you know what I discovered? (What's the matter,
you're not in the bathtub, are you? Well then, you
can damn well listen for a minute, surely, can't you?)
I discovered last night that all of my so-called friends
are sycophants. Of course, I'm not including *you*!
You're not a friend, sweet Jesus no, you're an arm,
you're a vital organ, a part of me. I breathe through
you, you silly, tiresome pussy. But the others! Roberta,
can you name me *one* who would have been there last
night if I were someone other than Kayo Hathaway,
creator of Bad Bad Jo-Jo? No, no, don't try. If it
weren't for the fact that my Jo-Jo books are in every
drugstore and my name in lights on half of the world's
movie theaters, that room would've been empty. Hesketh was right, you know. He said Bad Bad Jo-Jo made
Double-O-Seven seem as heavy-handed and old-fash-
ioned as Sherlock Holmes, and I must say he's right.
D'you know, Roberta, Jo-Jo still amuses me—far more
than any of my friends do, certainly. The very idea just
kills me: this dreadful, grinning little saint of a woman,
and this ghastly monster of a son, running through the
world like a dose of salts. You know, it is terribly funny, darling. "Bad, Bad!" she says, as Jo-Jo slaughters
twenty-two Communists before breakfast . . . How did
I get off on that? Oh, yes, Hesketh. Do you know what
else Hesketh said to me last night? He said, "You
know, Kayo, you might have been a *real* writer if you
hadn't been born with such a genius for trivia." Oh,
Hesketh is vicious. But it's not just Hesketh, it's all of
them. I had quite a sobering moment on my way home,
in the solitary splendor of my Carey Cadillac. Kayo,

said I, you are completely a-lone. Completely. So, darling Roberta, you see that I shall be no more alone in Switzerland than I am in America. What do you mean, have I had second thoughts? About leaving? I should say not! I'm getting out! And if you were smart, you'd listen. Something dreadful is going to happen here, and I don't want to be around when it does. . . . In America! That's where! I don't know, pet, but it's something foul. I can smell it. The stench of it is everywhere, it rises like fumes from the gratings in the streets, it lurks in doorways, it's the unwritten story on every front page. Nobody knows what it is, and yet everyone has a name for it. The liberals call it the John Birch Society, and the Birchers call it Communism. The white man says it's Black Power, the Negroes say it's the fuzz, the fuzz says it's the marijuana smokers. Meanwhile the poor dear potheads blame it all on the liquor lobbies. And Kayo Hathaway, well, he's just dizzy and terrified. My dear, I tell you, the hounds are snapping at our asses. Don't *you* feel it, Roberta? Well, I don't think it's exaggerated at all! Would you care to hear what I dreamed last night? I dreamed I was Marie Antoinette! And I trust you recall what happened to her fair white neck!

(*The doorbell rings.*)

Oh, Christ, there's the door. Who can it be? What time is it? Am I expecting someone? *Don't* hang up! Don't you dare, till I can think who it is. (*He rummages through notes on his desk.*) Roberta, did you make an appointment for me and forget to write it down? Oh, I know! It's someone from a fan magazine. It's not *Silver Screen,* and it's not *Photoplay,* but it's one of those. (*He picks up the house phone.*) Harris? Who is it? *Two* young men! No, I will not see two, I made an appointment with one. Send *one* up. (*He hangs up the house phone and goes to the door, leaving it ajar—still talking all the while to Roberta.*) Can you imagine? A personality interview with a writer, of all things, to be published in a movie magazine! Why, I don't even have any tits! . . . Roberta, couldn't you just chat with me till the young man comes? I *hate* being left completely alone.

(*Another phone rings.*)

Ha! There goes my other line. Apparently someone *wants* to talk to me. Goodbye. (*He hangs up.*) You hideous, selfish twat! (*He answers the second phone.*) Yes? Seymour? What's happening? Uh-huh, I see, well, here's my answer. You tell Miss Enormous Toosh that Mr. Hathaway is in an utter coma of pleasure, since she's consented to tour the barns in his poor little play. She's his favourite movie star in all the world. But then you whisper to her, Seymour, just whisper that between the two of you, Kayo Hathaway is totally unapproachable on the subject of money. If she wants more than ten per cent she'll have to get it from the producers.

(*During the above,* FRANK JONES *has entered. He is a large young man, with a powerful-looking body, but his manner is tentative, awkward, obsequious. This effect is so pronounced as to appear, at times, almost studied, and perhaps even vaguely disquieting. At the moment of his appearance,* KAYO *ushers him in with gestures.*)

Call me back and tell me what she says. I've got to go now, because I'm being rude to a perfectly delightful young man who has come to interview me for a fan magazine. And he has promised not to ask any questions about The Burning Issues Of The Day. Isn't that charming? All I've got to do, apparently, is tell whether or not I sleep in the raw. Are you titillated? Wait, wait! Don't hang up! Were you going to hang up on me? Oh, Seymour, don't ever hang up on me.

I want to ask you something very important. But hold on for one moment, while I tell my guest to make himself a drink. (*to* FRANK) Dear Guest, how do you do. (*They shake hands.*)

FRANK: Wow! I just shook hands with Kayo Hathaway! Wow-wee, am I ever impressed!

KAYO: Ha-ha, you do admire me, don't you. I love your being so forthright about it, how ingenuous. (*into phone*) Seymour! Are you clicking at me? Please, I will not be clicked at! (*to* FRANK) Help yourself at the bar. There's ice in the bucket. Now, apart from offering you a drink, and encouraging you to replenish it at your own discretion as the visit wears on, I will make no attempt whatever to put you at ease. If you're foolish enough to be nervous in the presence of my enormous celebrity—then that's your lookout, there's simply no relief for such obtuseness.

FRANK: I might've known you'd be, well, real down-to-earth and all.

KAYO: Down to what?

FRANK: Down to earth.

KAYO: Look around, if you like.

> (*While* KAYO *talks on the phone,* FRANK *looks around, inspecting the place with great interest. We might even see him reading a piece of mail, or listening on an extension phone in the hall. But he does not make himself a drink.*)

I want to know about the Swiss banks, have you checked on them yet? Oh, Seymour, god*damn*it, Seymour! I asked you weeks ago, I'm leaving in five days! Seymour, I'm extremely unhap— Oh, I beg your pardon, I thought you said you had *not* done it. Tell, tell! How much interest do they give? Ech, you call that interest? Well, if I can't do better . . . And listen, I've decided I want ten thou each in Palma, Gras, Tangier and Torremolinos. Then you'll put half of what's left of me in Swiss banks, and the other half in debentures. I do not want any growth stuff, understand? I am absolutely through with growth! I want security, and I want yield! I've earned what I've got and I intend to keep it. Oh, Seymour, I had the most brilliant notion, it came to me at three a.m., I almost phoned you then. Listen, I want you to tell Columbia that my European profits are to be placed directly into the Swiss bank—without *bothering* the United States Internal Revenue people. Have I made myself clear? If I'm going to be living abroad, not using these highways or breathing this polluted air, why in hell should I go on paying these exorbitant . . . Don't talk to me about illegal! This is 1969 and Richard Milltown Nixon is President: laws aren't something you obey, they're only there to be outwitted. Honestly, you frighten me. Whose side are you on? Oh, Christ, I just had a godawful thought! Seymour, are these Swiss bank accounts insured? Yes, but by whom? Oh, that's just fine and dandy, but what happens to me if Switzerland falls? Use that noodle, earn that fee! And phone me the minute you've talked with Nuestra Señora Del Culo Grande. . . . Our Lady Of The Big Butt, to you. (*As* KAYO *hangs up, he catches* FRANK *reading something on top of his desk.*) I did tell you to look around, didn't I!

FRANK: Gosh, I hope I didn't take any, well, you know, liberties! Because wow, I'm just—golly! So nervous anyway.

KAYO: Young man, there are three words in the American language which I abhor. They are Gosh, Wow, and Golly. You have already exceeded your quota of each of them.

FRANK: I just knew you'd have a sense of humor.

KAYO: That's where you cheapen yourself, I have none

whatever. Now, proceed with your questions, Mr.—
What is your name?

FRANK: Frank Jones.

KAYO: I'll call you Frank. Proceed with your questions,
Frank.

FRANK (*consulting notes*): What do you think of young
people today?

KAYO: You're kidding.

FRANK: I guess that sounded real dumb, huh?

KAYO: Is that your next question?

FRANK: Yeah, I guess it did. Gee, Mr. Hathaway . . .

KAYO: Remember what I said about *Gosh*, *Wow*, and
Golly? It also applies to *Gee*.

FRANK: Right, right! Well, see, I thought I'd ask your
opinions about various thing, because I was afraid it'd
be kind of impertinent to ask really personal questions.

KAYO: I adore personal questions. Why don't you ask me
why I'm leaving the country?

FRANK: Why are you leaving the country?

KAYO: To beat the income tax. Put that in your article.
I'm sick sick sick of supporting that endless, outra-
geously expensive tedium in Southeast Asia. And I'm
not a peacenik either. Are you?

FRANK: Me? Oh no. No, not at all.

KAYO: I hope not. I'm only against the war because it's
expensive! Some bearded little ass with a hideous com-
plexion came to me last week, said he'd heard I was
against the war and could he ask a few questions. The
first was a classic. He deplored, he said, the fact that
while Jean-Paul Sartre had gone to jail over the Al-
gerian question, no distinguished American author had
yet made such a bold stand against our own country's
atrocities in Vietnam. Could I tell him why? Me!
Well, I wasn't fooled for a moment, I knew full well
that in his damp, soiled little world, Kayo Hathaway

65

is regarded as the Whore of Babylon. Rich, successful, writes comedies, takes baths. I was being baited and I knew it. I said, Tell me, young man, why haven't you taken your Burning Questions to Tennessee Williams or Edward Albee, hmmm?

FRANK: Hah! Oh, that was great, great! What'd he say?

KAYO: He said that because my films had such a vast audience, I was the somethingest something in the world. King of Camp, I think it was. I thought that was actually rather sweet. His point seemed to be that while Edward and Tennessee win the laurels, Kayo wins the public imagination. And of course he's right. The public adores bloodshed and camp, because the public is a bloody camp, and that's what I give them. I give them themselves. I give them Jo-Jo and his mother, good-hearted murderers.

FRANK: Wow-wee! Excuse me, but Wow! That's fabulous. You really think the public is bloodthirsty?

KAYO: Oh, surely *that's* been established by now, hasn't it? The impotent are *always* obsessed with murder. And the public is impotent. Let me explain. The public is made up of a large number of individual persons who do not like or respect or trust one another. Therefore it has no hope of solidarity, and solidarity is its only power. Ergo, the public is impotent. It quite literally "can't get it up any more"! Hence, it amuses itself with bloodshed—making me a very rich man. However, I said none of this to my hippie interrogator, a very distasteful young man. No style, no *panache*.

(FRANK *is writing in his notebook.* KAYO *repeats the word for his benefit.*)

Pa-nache! A study in dreariness. He seemed bound and determined to make one feel that one's every public act was freighted with social consequence. I said, Young man, if I took you seriously I should never write another word. The only responsibility I accept is to amuse and titillate and astonish, and for one purpose only: to keep that lovely green river flowing across the box offices of the world—into my pocket. If in the process I should happen to give the poor, doomed public a moment's comic relief from both the anti-Communists and the anti-anti-Communists— one's as tiresome as the other, you know—I feel I shall have earned one tiny gold star in Heaven.

FRANK: Right, right!

KAYO: In a sense of course I'm deeply indebted to both. If it weren't for Peking there'd be no bad guys, and if it weren't for the CIA there'd be no good guys. In which event there'd be no Kayo Hathaway.

FRANK: Gosh, don't even say that!

KAYO: But to return to my hippie. You wouldn't have believed the impertinence. I'm certain he was a Communist, by the way. Communism always attracts the fuck-ups, the sour, angry little creatures who can't make their own way. I've always said that if religion is the opiate of the people, then Communism is the malingerer's dream of paradise. (*repeats, for* FRANK'*s benefit*) Mal-ing-er-er. Who knows, if I were lazy, or poor, or utterly talentless, I might be a Communist myself! Except, of course, that my intelligence, meager though it may be, is quite adequate for understanding a very simple natural law—namely, that nothing in the world is free. You get what you give.

FRANK: Oh? Oh, that's very interesting! Oh, golly, that's something I'd like to hear a lot more about. (*He writes.*) "You get what you give."

KAYO: Why are you writing that down?

FRANK: Well, frankly, it's just exactly the kind of thing I'd hate to forget. Tell me, sir, do you really believe it's true?

KAYO: Of course I do. But I can't believe you're really so impressed.

FRANK: Oh, but I am. You see, a person in your position obviously has some key, some philosophy that makes him so . . . successful. And of course that's what readers like to know about. Me too. I like to know, too.

KAYO: You said your name was Frank, didn't you?

FRANK: Yes, sir. Frank Jones.

KAYO: Um. Frank.

FRANK: Yes, sir.

KAYO: Frank, tell me. Why are you acting such a fool?

FRANK: Whee! Did you ever hit the nail right on the old head that time! I am a fool.

KAYO: My, my, my my my my my my my my MY! You're agreeable.

FRANK: Agreeable. Listen, do you want to hear the honest-to-god truth? I'm not agreeable, not at all. Not usually. But with you I feel like, gee, this is me talking. It's like listening to my own thoughts. Everything you say is just, wow, right on the old button.

KAYO: Mm-hm. I see. (KAYO *looks.* FRANK *perspires.*) You're with a magazine called what?

FRANK: *Image.*

KAYO: Oh, yes. *Image.* Why does *Image* want an interview with me, Frank? I'm not even pretty.

FRANK: But gosh, you're so famous, and you must know all the stars.

KAYO: Frank. Frank, you haven't said one interesting word since you walked in that door, and yet you have me absolutely fascinated.

FRANK: Oh, but I'm so boring. We shouldn't be talking about me.

KAYO: What do you want from me? Apart from this silly interview?

FRANK: Want?

KAYO: Yes. Want.

FRANK: Well, you're right, of course. I could be interviewing just any famous show-business person. But I've got this kind of fix on you. I had to see you, I had to hear you talk. I guess, mainly, I just wanted to be sure you were, well, *real!*

KAYO: No, dear boy, that won't do. You're not just a fan. You're restless. Restless people always want something. And in your case, it's something specific.

FRANK: Specific?

KAYO: Very. You want me to read a manuscript you've written. Is that it?

FRANK: Me, oh gosh, I can't write.

KAYO: Oh? But I thought you wrote for a living?

FRANK: Just hack stuff. But I'm no good or anything.

KAYO: Your eyes are quick. I suspect you're intelligent. And yet somehow it suits your, whatever it is, to play the fool.

FRANK: You give me way too much credit, Mr. Hathaway. Not that I think I'm real dumb. But intelligent? Nobody's ever accused me of that before! (*He laughs.*) Do you know something? I'm beginning to get an inkling. Just a kind of an inkling of what it is you noticed about me.

KAYO: Do go on.

FRANK: But I'm afraid you'll, well, laugh at me like.

KAYO: I assure you I will not.

FRANK: It's about . . . souls.

KAYO: Souls?

FRANK: Is that word too dumb?

KAYO: Not at all, it's intriguing.

FRANK: Well, I don't have all kinds of words like you do, so it's awfully hard for me to tell you what I mean.

KAYO: But you must try.

FRANK: I think we're . . . kindred souls. Is that a fairly pushy thing to say? I suppose it is.

KAYO: I'll let you know when I hear more. In what way are we kindred?

FRANK: When I read your books, or see your movies or

69

plays, I feel like I know exactly how you feel . . . about life and all.

KAYO: About life! Dear boy, I write nothing but gory, campy melodramas. Now please, I abhor flattery. Compliments are lovely, but they mustn't be empty.

FRANK: But I honestly do feel that my fate is connected with yours, in some real close way.

KAYO: How?

FRANK: How?

KAYO: Yes. How?

FRANK: Listen, I want to ask you a fantastic favor: Would you let me answer that question just a tiny bit later on?

KAYO: You feel that . . . your fate and mine are very closely related. Is that what you want to talk about a tiny bit later on?

FRANK: Yes, sir, because I've got to, you know, feel my way into it, into this talking about it. So far, it's only been a feeling. And if you'd just talk to me some more, about other things, I think it'd help a really awfully lot.

KAYO: You think it'd help a "really awfully lot," do you? And what would you like to talk about now?

FRANK: Well, I was just fantastically interested a while ago when you were talking about the public being bloodthirsty. Anything to do with murder is just fascinating to me.

KAYO: Would you like to give me three fingers of Scotch and the teensiest splash of soda. No ice.

FRANK: Sure. (*at the bar*) I can't believe it. I'm making a drink for Kayo Hathaway.

KAYO: You neither drink nor smoke, do you, Frank?

FRANK: I take a drink once in a while. But not today.

KAYO: Today's very special, isn't it?

FRANK: Gee, is it ever!

KAYO: I could have done without the "gee."

FRANK: Right! Right! I hate people t' say Gee. What makes me do that? (FRANK *hands* KAYO *the drink.*)

KAYO: Your hand is shaking.

FRANK: That's because I'm so mad at myself, saying all these dumb things, Gee this and Golly that.

KAYO: O-o-o-o-o-oh, Gawd!

FRANK: What is it?

KAYO: I just had a dreadful thought, I have virtually frightened myself half to death with it, in fact.

FRANK: What, what?

KAYO: I've allowed you to remain here because I imagined there might be something faintly interesting about you. But what, oh God, what shall I do if it develops that you're just as hopelessly dreary as you appear to be. The thought alone is enough to make me *gasp!*

FRANK: I'm sorry, I'm really sorry, honest.

KAYO: The thing I find most tedious of all is this constant apology. Couldn't we dispense with it?

FRANK: Right, sure, absolutely. It's just that I know what rotten company I am, and I'm just sorry that—whoops, there I go apologizing again. I'm sorry. Oh, gee, *again!*

KAYO: Perhaps if we change the subject. Back to your interview, hm?

FRANK: Fine, fine. Now, about this terrific statement of personal philosophy—I have it right here—"You get what you give." Beautiful. I was just wondering if you ever worry about that, though. I mean, about getting what you give?

KAYO: Worry?

FRANK: Yes, sir. I mean, doesn't the idea ever bother you?

KAYO: What the hell are you talking about, does the idea ever *bother* me; it's made me rich and famous, you fool!

FRANK: Oh.

KAYO: Oh, what? You really are peculiar. I'd give a whole

bagful of nickels to know what goes on in that head of yours.

FRANK (*straining after a thought*): You get what you give. See, I was thinking that if what you give to the world are these wonderfully campy murders, then maybe you'd be afraid that what the world would give back would be—well, the same thing!

KAYO: What in God's name does that mean?

FRANK: It's just—I wondered if you've ever been afraid of being—killed—in some wonderfully campy way?

KAYO: My! My, my! Whoopee! Goodness sake! And hibbety-bibbety-bobbety-ZIP! You have come through with an original thought! I'll bet you have all sorts of ideas tucked away in there, don't you.

FRANK: Oh, gosh, sir, I don't have any ideas. I've just got all this crap, I mean, excuse me, junk in my head and I'm, well, I'm just a young, nutty guy trying to get his thoughts kind of sorted out. You know. So I say all this dumb stuff.

KAYO: Dear boy, I give the public entertainment. The public is king—a fat, disgusting king without power and without balls, as I've pointed out. But it does have money. And I am one of its grotesquely overpaid court jesters. Is it really and truly necessary to point out to you that I do not kill people? I am in show business.

FRANK: Oh, boy, have I ever made a fool of myself. I been trying to make you think I'm this great thinker or something. I suppose it's because I admire you so tremendously, and it's hard for me to be my, well, my*self*, around somebody of your fantastic stature. Does that make any sense to you?

KAYO (*bored*): I told you at the outset there'd be very little I could do to reduce that barrier.

FRANK: Well, I suppose the least I can do now is, you know, like *leave*.

(KAYO *waves bye-bye*.)

After having fallen completely on my face. Wow-*wee*, I really do disgust myself. (*starts to leave*) I just want you to know I wouldn't be nearly so dumb around, say, Tennessee Williams or Andy Warhol!

KAYOS (*appalled*): Andy Warhol!

FRANK: Or anybody else. But you, you're the really, well, you know, like the Great Man. And—okay, okay. Excuse me. I'm going now. (*at the door*) Oh! Oh gosh! Oh wow! I forgot! I can't go down there now. He'll never forgive me.

KAYO: Who will never forgive you for what?

FRANK: It's this friend. He's in the lobby. He's waiting down there, and I just don't know how to face him after lousing everything up.

KAYO: Oh, come now, I'm sure you haven't acquitted yourself quite so shabbily as all that. And if you have, the marks of it are not tattooed on your face. You could lie, couldn't you? Pretend you were brilliant?

FRANK: You don't understand! I promised him!

KAYO: Promised him what?

FRANK: Well, it's . . . No, no, I can't ask you a favor now. This is my own problem, I'll just have to . . . get through it myself. Goodbye, sir.

KAYO (*curious*): Oh, come now, what is this all about? What favor did you want to ask of me? If it's so unthinkable, I can assure you I'm quite capable of refusing.

FRANK: Well, it's this: this friend is just a great guy, you know? His name is Dennis. He's a terrific kind of goofy, wonderful little guy. And he's just as hung up on you as I am. He hoped you'd say Hi to him.

KAYO: Hi?

FRANK: I guess you think that's pretty repulsive kid stuff, right?

KAYO: (*grandly weary*): Where is he?

FRANK: You mean you're going to let him come up?

KAYO: Of course. Dear heaven, I thought you were going to ask for an arm, or an eyetooth.

FRANK: Oh, nothing like that.

(KAYO *picks up the house phone, clicks the hook.*) Wow! Dennis is going to get such a thrill. You can't imagine what this'll mean to him.

KAYO: I have a fair idea.

FRANK: Oh no, you don't.

KAYO (*into phone*): Harris? Harris, there's a young man down there. Let him come up.

FRANK: Oh, Mr. Hathaway, you're making two crazy, unimportant little guys awful happy this afternoon. Honest.

KAYO: Perhaps you'd like to know why I'm bothering.

FRANK: If you'd care to tell me, I'd love to hear.

KAYO: Sheer curiosity. I'm wondering if your friend can be half as disgusting as you are.

FRANK (*laughing appreciatively*): Oh, that's great!

KAYO: I *thought* you'd like that!

FRANK: Wow, I'll say! You just come out with whatever you're thinking. It's fabulous!

KAYO: Why don't you get down on your knees to me? That's what you really want to do, isn't it?

(FRANK *drops to his knees.*)

Ho-ho, I see! I'm a full-fledged god now, aren't I? I order you *not* to kiss my feet, I have a weak stomach. Get up.

(A *buzzer is heard.*)

FRANK: May I get the door?

KAYO: Please do.

(FRANK *opens the door.*)

FRANK: Come on in, Dennis, and meet the greatest guy in the world, Kayo Hathaway. Mr. Hathaway, this is Dennis.

(DENNIS *is small, skinny, adenoidal, probably a user of dexedrine or amphetamine. He moves*

like the sort of creature who lives in dark under-
ground places. He is carrying a shopping bag.)

DENNIS: Oh, Mr. Hathaway, I'm dumbfounded, I'm absolutely nonplused and stupefied. I've got this whole
speech prepared and I'm just too flabbergasted to—
What can I say except "Gosh!"

KAYO: You might've tried "Gee Whiz."

DENNIS: Frank, did you ask him?

FRANK: You mean if we could . . . ? Oh, golly I didn't have
the nerve.

DENNIS: Well, I'm going to blurt it right out. Mr. Hathaway, we want to show you our act. Not because we
think it's any good or anything, but it'd be our little
present to you, who've given the world so much. See,
I do this imitation of Mama, and he does Bad Bad
Jo-Jo, and our friends think we're very funny. So
could we?

KAYO: Oh *please* do.

> (DENNIS *puts on a lady's hat, a furpiece, tiny eye-*
> *glasses, and snaps a chain onto* FRANK's *belt*
> *buckle.* FRANK, *leashed now, with an under-sized*
> *Uncle Sam hat on his head, takes an apelike*
> *stance, and the two of them strike a pose under*
> *the* Bad Bad Jo-Jo *lobby poster, managing to*
> *look amazingly like it.* KAYO, *easily seduced by*
> *this enactment of his own creation, watches with*
> *pleasure.* DENNIS *speaks now in a little-old-lady*
> *voice.*)

DENNIS: G'd afternoon, Mr. Hathaway. Has my Jo-Jo been
botherin' you somethin' awful? He can be a real nui-
sance and don't I know it. But he's goodhearted, they's
nothin' Jo-Jo wouldn't do for a friend. Or his mama.
Or his country, or God. Them four: Mama, God,
country and friend. Why, Jo-Jo knew the Pledge of
Allegiance when he was three. He wandered away from
his mama in a department store one day, and they took

him to the lost-kiddies' department. The lady asked
him, What's your name, little boy, and where do you
live? And Jo-Jo said, I pledge allegiance to the flag of
the United States of America. Isn't that sweet? Didn't
know who he was—but he knew the stars and stripes
of his Uncle Sam. (*vaudeville tears*) Oh, I was s'proud.
Say the rest of it for Mr. Hathaway, Jo-Jo. "And to
the republic for which it stands." Go ahead.

Jo-Jo: One nation under God, with liberty and justice for
all.

Mama: Liberty and justice for all, except?

Jo-Jo: Except Commies and hippies and faggots and niggers
and peace creeps.

Mama: And? Sympathizers! You always forget the sympathizers, and they're the worst of all! Oh, how nice,
thank you, Mr. Hathaway, a cup of tea'd be ever-so-
nice. Or whiskey, if it's easier. Yes, I think a cup of
whiskey'd be lovely.

Kayo: Now look, you boys have amused me enormously,
you truly have, but now I think . . . !
(*He touches his watch.*)

Mama: Oh, don't you go frettin' yourself about time,
honey, I got all the time in the world. Jo-Jo, bring
y'mommy a nice warm cup o' Scotch, she feels a chill.
(*Jo-Jo goes to the bar, pours.*)

Kayo (*tapping his watch*): Look, I'm terribly serious about
this.

Mama: What's that, son? Is it your watch that's botherin'
you? What's wrong with it, does it itch?

Kayo: Now I'm afraid you're forcing me to be heavy-
handed.

Mama: Let me see that watch, honey.
(*Jo-Jo hands Mama a glass of whiskey.*)
Oh, thank you, darlin'. (*She swallows it in a gulp.
Then, to Kayo*) Hand it to Mama.
(*Pause. Kayo is frightened now.*)

Jo-Jo. Fetch me that watch Mr. Hathaway's got on his wrist.

(Jo-Jo *easily removes the watch from* KAYO, *who is more and more docile with fear.*)

Mr. Hathaway doesn't know what a temper it puts Mama into, having one of her boys go disobedient on her like that. I think he ought to have a smart little slap.

(Jo-Jo *slaps* KAYO.)

KAYO: How dare you! You don't work for a magazine at all. You're nothing but a . . .

MAMA: Nothin' but a what, honey? Oh, goodness, now I know what's troublin' Mr. Hathaway. He thinks you're a robber, Jo-Jo. He thinks we've come to steal his watch.

KAYO: I wish you boys would take what you want—and leave.

MAMA: Y'see? I was right. Here, Jo-Jo, take this watch and throw it out the window. Then he'll know we're here in good faith!

(Jo-Jo *obeys.*)

KAYO: All right then. What do you want?

MAMA: Do you know what I think, Jo-Jo? I think Mr. Hathaway's a Commie. I felt somethin' funny the minute I come in here. What do you suppose he created characters like us for in the first place? Why, he's trying to make fools out of the plain, honest folk that tries to rid this old world of the Reds. I won't stand for it! Okay, mister, I'm giving you a fair and square deal. Are you a Commie?

(*The phone rings.*)

Ha! The telephone! See? He's trying to change the subject! Pull that cord out, Jo-Jo.

(*Now there is a marked increase in tempo. As* Jo-Jo *pulls the telephone cord,* MAMA *withdraws two tiny folded squares of plastic from her shop-*

ping bag, handing one to Jo-Jo. *They unwrap the articles, and we see that they are raincoats.*)

Here, son, put this on. These are wonderful little things, Mr. Hathaway. Jo-Jo thought of them. Mama, he said, if we put these on at Mr. Hathaway's house, we won't get any on us. Wasn't that clever?

KAYO: Won't get any—what—on you?

JO-JO: Blood.

(Jo-Jo *and* MAMA *laugh fiendishly.*)

KAYO: Listen to me, I'm a very rich and powerful man. You'll never get away with—whatever it is you plan to do. But if you stop, I can get you anything you want. Anything. I also have a—an appreciation of this sort of—wit. It's maniacal, of course, but it's also very clever, and stimulating, and—and if the joke stops at once, I'll see to it you're both well rewarded—for the— for amusing me—so profoundly!

MAMA: Oh, son, we couldn't stop now . . .

(Jo-Jo *has backed* KAYO *onto a pouf, downstage.* MAMA *hands* Jo-Jo *a large knife.*)

. . . we just couldn't. Why, if Jo-Jo and me was to quit, right in the middle of a commitment, we'd never be able to show our faces again.

(*The music of the nightmare is heard again now, and the lights are dimmed to black, as the two young men close in on* KAYO HATHAWAY. *The various stages of his murder, a deliberate, ritualistic event, are seen under the flashing lights of a stroboscope, while throughout the theater and on the walls of the set, a rapid succession of photographic blow-ups is projected: a policeman clubs a peace marcher; a GI stabs a Vietcong; an 007-type shoots someone in the face; soldiers burn an Oriental village; someone is mugged; blacks smash a store window; a close-up of Sirhan Sirhan; President Nixon waves and smiles; Tom-*

*my Smothers looks bewildered; Allen Ginsberg
prays.*

DENNIS *leans the body of* KAYO *against the* Bad
Bad Jo-Jo *poster, while* FRANK *places in front of
it an ornamental gold-leaf picture frame. The
two young men bow to one another.*)
                    Curtain